Poetry of Heart

Poetry of Heart

Nehemiah Dixon Jr.

To order additional copies of this book, contact:
Xlibris Corporation
1-888-795-4274
www.Xlibris.com
Orders@Xlibris.com
98854

CONTENTS

Happiness

I fathered the life of misery
She sleeps late in early morn
She has sweet honey milk and tea
Her hopes are scarred and torn

My neice is called curiosity
My nephew is loneliness
There is one who takes away my breath
They call her Happiness

If you find Happiness
Bring her to me
I've searched for her
Through land and sea
I long to hold her close and tenderly
Then bring to life her fantasy

If you find happiness
Show her to me
I've yet to see her face
Still I hear that she may be
In every kind of place
On country road and city street
I seek the maiden fair.
Surely to know her whence we meet
For joy are the colors that she bear

Happiness a treasure chest
All men do desire
Caress me with your loveliness
That I may have thee until I die

Challenger

Challenger, Challenger
  what future has America
Challenger
Did take off time-
Claim the lives of those so brave.
What cause would call those
Great ones, from glory to the grave-?
Pioneers in Space-
On journey toward the Stars-
Unknown to Man-
Yet a playground for God-
Postponed landing
Preserved a chosen few,
A blistfull ending
 courageous and true.
Still another challenge is on it's way!
Though man conquer the exspanse,
Wandering through the Galaxy.
Tomorrow's just another day,
The future belongs to the free.
We live here on earth-gazing at the sky
Challenging the universe,
                Challenger did fly.
        Valiantly it flew
Out of this Atmosphere
                it caused the rain to come.
Tears for a Thousand years,
                because of what was done

Only God knows, what happened up there?
He gave birds wings, to fly every where
Was this a grim message
Or was it pre-destined?
From labor to reward
 the challenger was called.
Leaving some greiving, others believing.
The order was tall, , with blessings from all
We don't know why
Challenger did die
With greif filled hearts
The world was shocked
When Challenger exploded
Moments after take off.
America must hold her banner high
As we fought for Earth
,we must fight for the Sky
This is only the beginning
For we challenge the Stars
There can be no ending
Untill we homestead Mars.
The crew of the Challenger
Shall always remain
In our hearts forever
Then space we will claim.
The first planet
We'll name after you
Challenge of the Challenger
Brave and true

Add A Blessing

Let us all come together
To worship in his name
While he takes away our pain
Then relieve us of the shame

For his mercy we shall claim
When we worship in his name
For his mercy we shall claim
Like sunshine after rain

Holiness clean and pure
With boldness we must secure
A crown's promised those who endure
Everlasting life definitely sure

All of our trials and tribulations
Merely trinkets of salvation
Charity; hope; faith and peace
Are the victories we seek
No longer will we have to weep
    or be challenged by defeat
We grow stronger
    with each command we keep
My heart's reserve through teaching his word
May the Lord add a blessing every time the spirit urge
May the Lord add a blessing to the reading of his word
May the Lord add a blessing to his word

Drugs For Dreams

How you disrespecT
me,
in my own crib.
took you off the street,
 gave you space to live.
Say you loveD
with all your heart
If true? I'd like to play the part.
Open your eyes,
what you're saying isn't real
you measure love only;
from lust you feel.
Any man loving you
would be always by your side.
More than kissing, hugging,
affectionately deprived.
what happened to the dreams
We used to share?
To me they were everything.
Passionate, extravagant,
delicacies so rare.
Dreadful thoughts enlisted care.
Lost in midnight delights
that bring despair.
Popularity
Was disguised as a friend.
Brought sudden tragedy
witnessed one life end.
Next door neighbor,
High school mate
Genocide, homecide
was the meal we ate.
How could I be victimized
by the call of the streets,
long before I recognize
fruits I would eat.

In order to survive
I sought victory in defeat
Our youth ostrasized
there was no one qualified
to advise
We have to come together
to make things better
Trust and create community pride
Exchange drugs for self love
make dreams
Real as they seem;
Educate, motivate, congregate
,it's never too late.

from city; to you
A pity; yet true
All authority upon the earth;,sea;,universe
Totaly belong to me;,even the galaxy

Time

Time please slow down for me
You're moving much to fast
Autumn breezes blow so free
Summer slipped right p a s t

Old age creeps so rapidly
Be fore you know it
She's come and gone
With only a memory
To linger on

Soon even thought shall desert
Her bones turn to ashes; soil
Spoils; peables in rain
What in the whole universe
Shall salvage man or give
Reconing from whence he came

So time please slow down for me
You're aging agelessly; drifting driftlessly
Like a wave upon the open sea
Searching, striving, seeking, sighing,
Trying desperately one day to be free

Time wont you be so kind
Erase the cobwebs from my mind
Let the sun light always shine
On the bright side of dreams devine

Eventually

Though stiff oposition
With tough competion
Control rigid restriction
Still I got permission
To swallow my sorrow;
Thus paved the way to
Addiction; but it was okay
Because the doctor
Was the author
Of my affliction
Orgerstrated the slaughter
Until it sought his daughter
Then the disease had to expand
Beyond the city into surburban
Suddenly no longer
Were my conviction smitten
Hooked by a legal crook
Like an eagle off I took
Which depiction of my admission
Had I listen to prediction
Prescription written "day of acquisition
Immediately everything I see is part of destiny
Time is mine relative only hope is devine
Refine thoughts behind
Imagine what may happen
If everybody had the ability to be
Simply wish for
There it exist at the door

Pills; Pills; Pills

A pill for drugs
One for kisses and hugs
A pill to laugh
                a pill to cry
A pill to bring you down
                a pill to get you high
A pill for the pain
                a pill for the lame
A pill to make u walk
                a pill to make you talk
A pill for love
                a pill for blood
A pill to laugh
                a pill for a bath
A pill to make you slow
                a pill to help you grow
A pill for the day
                a pill for the night
A pill for the weak
                a pill to give you might
                a pill to make you eat
A pill to lose your appetite
A pill for love
                a pill for drugs
A pill to laugh
                a pill to cry
A pill to make you sleep
                a pill to wake you up
A pill to get you high
                a pill to make you tough
A pill to make you sad
                a pill to make you glad
A pill to make you mad
                a pill to make you bad
Pills Pills Pills
                as long as you live

Revolution

Revolution is the solution
Revolutionized was characterized
            by thoughts of the idea
Of men willing to die
            than compromise the exspression
Of oppression and fear
            the people fail to see the need
Of total equality
They opened doors to scrub the floors
of a dying soceity
for selfish greed
Many hearts have had to bleed
            valiant and strong are songs
righteousness would sing
            a chosen few with thoughts brand new
Should magnify the dream
            millions have tried more have died
True freedom does not disguise
            the people fail to see the need
Of total equality
            they've opened doors
                        to scrub the floors
Of a dying society
      America to you I speak
                        from the pullpit
                                    of my soul
That which you stole
            you cannot keep
                        and continue being whole

Sleeping Giants

Brothers and sisters
                awaken and see
Your beautiful faith
                and destiny
Like sleeping giants
                you walk through the streets
Killing eacn other
                like flocks of sheep
Into the world you came
                you came full of reason
In time you came
                for the cotton season
Not knowing when
                where or what to do
Unwittingly you fell
                in the hands of taboo
So bad be you
                and all of your kind
While you kill each other
                from time to time
For you are here
                mearly a curse
I dread the thought
                of any thing worst
Than a brother
                to hate himself
Reasons unsolved
                so much as to kill
Within a family brawl
                only a few different and unique
Be proud of your selves
                with your rythmn and beat
You are the strongest
                beyond all the weak
Remember my brother
                the earth shall inherit the meek

Brooklyn Bridge

Brooklyn Bridge
               B r o o k l y n B r i d g e
Tons of iron and steel
               B r o o k l y n B r i d g e
   Brooklyn Bridge
            a thousand men to build
The eight wonder
            of the world
Man's victory
            a marvelous structure
Upon the land
            causing Brooklyn and
Manhatten to band
            miraculously the bridge acsends
A monument designed
            and refined by men
Thus the east river flows
              beneath gigantic stone
Peacefuly eminating
            while noisey moterist
Dispel the fish
            yet it stands in all magnificence
Through rain, snow, sleet
              deceit and hail
The bridge is built
            courageously well
Brooklyn Bridge
            Brooklyn Bridge
Tons of iron and steel
            Brooklyn Bridge
Brooklyn Bridge
            a thousand men to build

Incidental Affair

It was an incidental affair
All of the girls and the
fellows were there
Then you walked in
And my heart skipped a beat
Girl don't you know it fell to the flo
Your eyes glowed like stars so bright
Your smile showed you were mine for the night

It was an incidental affair
I remember the length
Of your hair
I fell so deep in love
 with you girl
Your lips so sweet
That's when I gave you the world
 touched your hand you made me your man
Fate has a plan we may not under stand

It was an incidental affair
Now my life is yours to share
Don't let no one separate this
 love we've found
After all is said and done
If you fall I'll be around
No I'll never let you down

Ask Somebody About Jesus

Why don't you walk with God
Why don't you talk with God
Why don't you ask somebody
         about J----e---s----u---s
Once I was lost in sin
Seemed like my life would end
Then I found hope in the name
         of S---a—l—v---a—t—i—o—n
So many times I tried
To find some good in life
But mostly they jived
Then gave me bad advice
Until I got so tired
Even alone I cried
Till I was sick inside
The whole world denied
Everything I desired
Finally in despair I kneeled down in prayer
And since that day God came to show me the way
Now I know that christ sacrificed his life
So all who believe can live sin free
As you walk with the Lord
Your day won't be so hard
Cause you can see spiritually
Yes we have the V----i----c---t----o----r----y

Why don't you walk with God
Why don't you talk with God
Why don't you ask somebody
         about J----e------s------u------s

Africa

I long to be in Africa
                    to lay all day in the sun
I would play in the jungle
                    from dusk until the dawn come
Whence I feel the warmth
                    glaze upon my brow
I will dig into earth;
                    my hand the plow
My motherland, utopia!
                    where my blood does run
I long to be in Africa
                    where the soil is rich and dark
The place where my ancestors are from;
                    amiss nature's heart
A place God would come
                    /where life did start
I long to be in Africa
                    /source of rare gold
So my spirit can be at liberty
                    /beauty of soul
I long to be in Africa/
                    to feel hot wind blow
Birthplace of diamonds
                    /preciously rare to behold
To watch the leaves
                    /dance in the trees
I'll be at ease/
                    when I see the Euphrates
There creation began
                    where God blew breath in to man
I long to be in Africa;
                    /barefeet in the sand
Roots of truth await
                    /just to shake my hand
Seeds of greed brought forth/
                    weeds who decieve

They would feed upon treasure
                    /took our wealth
Stole luxuries and pleasure
                    /infected our health
At liberty with diseases/
                    without any remendy
Stripped the earth
                    of minerals irreplaceble
Killed some at birth/
                    rapped and maimed,
        with no shame
                    ostracized my name

Fast Fast Fast

Don't let me pass you lady
Else it could be too late
I stopped to ask if maybe
You might be going my way

I'm running fast; fast; fast
I gotta keep up the pace
I'm runinng fast; fast; fast
I gotta win this race

Don't let me speed right by
I come to please satisfy
Can you understand!
I want to play the part
I'll write a song upon your heart
I want to be your man

I'm running fast; fast; fast
I gotta keep up my speed
I'm running fast; fast; fast
I gotta keep my lead
Don't let me speed ahead
My many passions must be fed
All of the time
Emotions run so deep
I offer joy that you may keep
The rest of your life

I really dig your smile
I'm even big on your style
Will you be as nice
Yeah you look so fine
But are you just as kind
Then you got to be mine
All of the time

I just stopped to tell you baby
That other guy he loves you maybe
My desire transpire to let you know
This hope I declare shall never go

Should you need someone for real
Come and feed on the love you feel
True hearts beat the same each day
No soul control the game sheep play

You And I

How would you like

to ride a kite

Up in the sky

so high

Oh baby, just you and I

for million s of miles

We'll get a hitch

on a cloud

Honey you know I try

see all the neat things I buy

sweety just you and me

together eternally

Is it that hard to see

you are my candy tree

What would you say

if you got your pay

Saw it's a half a day short

would you go to your boss

Tell'em off

or would you take 'em to court

Baby just you and I

watching the world floating by

Baby just you and me

in reality

Fin e as you wanna be

you can only be kind

My ddesire is designed

loving you through your mind

When I first saw your face

put me in a trance

I never knew love's embrace

hooked from a glance

Perhaps all of this

is some strange dream

If so then I wish

I awake crowned a king

How would you like

        to ooh ride a kite

Up in the sky

        so high

Nothing on earth

        could mean as much

I hunger and thirst

        lust for your touch

Others have tried

        to feed and provide

Only you satisfy

I'll Make You Mine

What ever your pleasure
          what ever your heart desire
Girl I'll bring you treasure
          girl I'll make you mine
So when you see me
          walking down the street
Girl you just walk on by
          you don't hear me speak
Girl you make me wanna cry
If I had a genie
          who would make all my dreams
Come true
          I'd trade them all for just one chance
To spend a moment with you
          patience is a virtue
Good things come
          to those that wait
               your soul I'd nurture
Until it's my turn
          to stand at heaven's gate
So whatever your pleasure
          whatever your heart desire
Girl I'll bring you treasure
          girl I'll make you mine

Jesse Ray

Hey did you hear about brother Jesse Ray?
Yeah we heard, he got killed on on the block today.---
Tell me brother, just what did he do
Stole a loaf of bread and bolongny too_---
Heard he was shot six times
Left a wife and five kids behind
What happened to cause his demise and defeat?
He was broke and his family needed to eat.
Why did'nt the brother get a job
He was trying but times is just that hard
People from other countries got more breaks than us
Born poor in America makes it twice as rough
Sell drugs and go to jail
Rob a bank and go to hell
Go to school and get an education
Over qualified for the situation
It's just another brother laid to rest
Make you wonder who can pass the test
Can you sing, dance, or play sports
Plenty of room for all that sort
Other wise it's homecide and genocide
Put drugs in the street watch'um drop like flies
So they'll leave our stores alone
Get them hooked on something worst than heroine
Tell me bro-I think you got it wrong
They trying to help giving us methedone
Tell me brother when you drink tomorrow
Check out the poison lable on the bottle
Some make it those who really tried
For every one that got over ninety nine died

Girl

Girl you're gonna come to me
When the stars above you no longer see
Then there will only be
Light provided by my company
Will set you free
And make ue we

Girl you're so very rare
When I see you there
I declare you're the answer
To a rich man's dream
A poor man's prayer

Girl you're the one I need
Every breath I breathe
You're the precious seed
Upon luciousness beauty feeds
Each caress emotions bleed
Seek success selection squeeze
Reject reflections of passions greed

Then we can be together eternally
That which predestine us to be

Abandoned

I thought we shared a love wish-
Suddenly we were drawn apart—
Yet in the middle, joy was switched
Nothing is sadder than broken hearts
I stored my soul in our mixed emotions
Marvelous as gold, stiched silver devotion
I need to feed hunger's request
Please ease these teased feelings of loneliness
Only you could capture intimate desire
Exchange hate for a taste of happiness
You've conjured a place as hot as fire
Once fair a delightful treasure
Unaware you sought another's pleasure
Leaving me in total bliss
How could fate share sadness
What affection missed
I sought to repair madness
My pledge to love forever
You said you felt the same
Mother disaproved the endeavor
Still you would bare my name
Ten years of heartache and tears
Could eternity erase thy shame
Somehow I destroyed
 the love you loaned to me
This moment it's void
Of all that use to be
I gave you everything
That I ever owned
Made you my queen
Right now I'm alone
The love that brought sunshine
In the middle of winter snow
Now lost in the wheels of time
Somewhere, someplace
We use to know

Cheater's Heart

Once true love was in your eye
yet jealousy told you a lie
Now nothing can ever satisfy
The passion you let slip by it's over
I feel like I lost a four leaf clover
There is nothing greater than
The love of a woman and a man
You had everthing in you hand
Too complexive to understand
All you had to do was be true
Beauty can't even compare
To the thought of one who care
Real love wll always share
Use to get real fly catch um by surprise
I caught his girl when she looked in my eyes
This aint nothing new to thine own self be true
The first play of the day is knowing what to say
Turning nothing into gold good for the soul
Take a cripple philly how to run
On the track day and night till I catch one
Saw her watching me I knew she was ready to flee
Why be wid a sucker when she can be wit me
He can't keepa she a theif and a creeper
I ain't met one yet that wasn't a cheater
Even the girl I gave my name
Stole my world left me in shame
I thought I was strong in the game
She broke my heart all the way into
Said it was for somebody new
I gave her everthing I had
But it was too late to eradicate
Gave her money and luxury
She said all she wanted was me

Circus Girl

I always wanted a girl in the circus world
I always wanted a love of my own
I always wanted a girl from the circus world
A sweet thiing I could take straight home

    I met her under
               the big tent a rainny afternoon
I said lady wait
               one moment I've got love for you
She didn't believe that
                  my love was true
I said hey lady
               why do you think I'm blue
I always wanted a girl from the circus world
I valways wanted a girl of my own
I always wanted a girl from the circus world
A sweet thing I could take straight home
Each time I see you
               pass by me, my heart conspire
My mind wants to
               grasp, thy dark desire
Should chance ever
               allow such a treasure to infiltrate my life
Would romance clever
               some how trust pleasure enough to negociate the price
I will capture the wind
               blow sweet and freash
Again and again
               so deep I'd caress
Whatever would bring you joy
               that is my gift to you
Better good things employ
               a match, I killed habbits it's true

Come Back/Reality

Please get down on your knees
Say a prayer; be releived
I want you to be aware indeed
Of the air you breathe
Time is moving so far you losing
Try to relate to somehing else
Take pride in your self
See if you can stand like a man
All these years all these fears
What happened to your family
Kids are big they don't dig
Desertion
You upset they don't call; come see,
Asertion
No power; thy seed devour
They use to cry
You didn't come by
Now you wonder why
No phone calls no birthday cards
Nobody care how you fare
When you had the world in you hands
Had a royal flush didn't understand
Now the shoe on the other foot
Suck it on down look what they took
Can't nobody help untill you open your eyes
Find that spirit to revive what's inside
Wake up you slept lone enough
It's time for you to get up
Life is too precious
To throw it away
The greatest connection
Kneel down and pray
Your family need you to get it together
Stop waisting time you can do better
A shame what happened to so many folks
Got hooked on heroin mixed with coke

They called it speedball guess what it did
Caused millions to fall killed thousands of kids
They say that the FBI was down with the plan
Straight up genocide paralyse the poor man
Tried to keep it strictly uptown
It spread like wildfire, suburban bound
I asked my friend to credit me a bag
Until my package came
He said no, cause if he had I'd be out of the game

Hey Lady

I just stop to tell you baby
That other guy he love you maybe
Then again I'm here to let you know
This love i have will never go

If you need a love for real
I'll give you love you can feel
This kind of love is not for play
The love i share will always stay

Some folks like to kiss and hug
Come too and fro wish and plug
A passion for lust

I guess it was a school boy's crush

Come My Love

How you doing
                you mighty pretty
I don't even
                know your name
I'd like to know you better
    if you're not a shame
Of things you feel in side
    only love can claim
My passion and desire
    you've never met a guy like me
My petition for love is rare
    I don't have any luxeries
Though many treasures
                we can share
They call it roses and wine
                freash summer breeze
They call it pleasantness
                on a spring day eve
They call it warm and tender
                and very sweet
They call it splendor
                to cherish and keep
If I'm out of place
                please tell me so
Maybe I'll never taste
                your gentle lips even though
I will dream and imagine
 the way life would be
When things I'm after
                become reality
Then you will see
                what you've never seen before
Love is not a fantasy
                it's knocking at your door
Come my love in mid day
                or mid of night

Come to me my my love
          that you may see the light
When you have felt the need
          and caught all you want
Then come to me and feed
          until our love unites as one

Dogonit It

It's a shame trapped off;
            cause I'm late in the game
Ain't got nothing to claim
            not even weight to hold my name
It's getting harder to make it
            watching information on tv
Thinking maybe I can fake it
Getting colder than cold
Crack trapped off
            what use to be hoes
Pimping kinda slow
            tough without no dough
Ain't been paid so long
            feel like I played my whole life wrong
Time you can't take back
            once you use it you lose it
Best to check it right
   no second chances
            when you have no delight
In the hood
            how you gone do good
Everybody like you
            only one you can turn to
He alone can relieve us
Nobody else you can trust
            he won't deceive us
His name is Jesus, Jesus, Jesus
Will he allow me to sufer
            until I discover the correct way
A battle deep in my soul
            my heart wanna take control
I'm crying can't nobody hear
            sighing but can't shed a tear
When my life is together
            price is a ticket to do better
Been struggling doing bad

       gotta pray every day
Take care, share; forget
       what you had
Lost my dignity and pride
       sold my dreams for a puff and a hag
Thought I found hope in a ten cent bag
       I confess I made a mess
       misuse of my time
Gotta kick this habit
       that's destroying my mind
Let me be a wacthman of truth
I know I can bring forth proof
Lord forgive me
       set me free
From everthing
       contrary to thee
m ake me a soldier of righeoustness
       let me be forever blessed
Guide, protect direct me Lord
Life aint really got to be so hard

Dream

I Dream someday that I will play
Where cherry blossoms grow
Where april showers come in may
Where warm soft breezes blow

I Dream tonight in pure delight
That man in time will see
There is no reason to fuss and fight
That love is all we need

I dream of life as that pot of gold
All seekers hope to find
All minerals of life are in the soul
All riches are in the mind

I Dream of death as an unpaid debt
When light of day must end
The price you pay is already set
The new birth of earth begins

Dream Dream tell me
What you mean
Last night I sat upon a throne
And loved a Virgin Queen

Princess Dye

Princess Dye — I — know — that — I
                                    — only saw you from a far
Wheather on the surface of land
                                    or the heavenly exspanse
Your essence will always shine
                                    brighter than the highest star

Millions love and admire your lovely face
Quiet beautiful illustrious and fare
I'm sure God reserved a glorioue place
Where undisturbed pure hearts share

How could — you — know —
                                    you'd be chosen by destiny

That you would have honor
                                    to bring life to a king

To live in all the luxury
                                    most people dare to dream

Who cast the lot the world was shocked
You employed a wonderful life
There are some things that can't be bought
Can't be purchased at any price

Only God has power to recocile
                                    thousands wept because you died
Though one bear riches undefiled
                                    wealth profit unreconized
Whence nature breath exspired
Since diamonds, silver even gold
No stay can delay what is required
Hence death commands your soul

Though benelvolence---reveal
                                    secrets kept in royalty

Dianna's residence---killed
                                    by precepts of society

Heavenly Father

Heavenly father hear my prayer
make it a better world
For me somewhere
people come down on their knees
But what they're looking for
ain' t nothing but greed
They look for silver
diamonds and gold
None off these things Lord
can save their soul;
They need Jesus and his rightousness
He is the one who died,
that all might be blessed

Heavenly father; come in my life
Give me your will Lord to do what is right
Save me from sin Lord, and all wickedness
Please let me win Lord instill your holiness

First change my thoughts Lord,
Teach me to love; Lord to understand
Your gift of the blood, that you gave to man

I need the power cherished the most
Feed and shower me with the holy ghost
People are dying out in the street
Children are crying for something to eat

Heavenly father don't pass me by
Send your spirit that never die
Lord you promised eternal life
You are my anchor in you i delight
Heavenly father hear my prayer-
Make it a better world-for me somewhere

Hippie

There's a hippie
                    standing on the corner
Singing songs
                    to the people passing by
There's a man in jail
                        cause society failed
And they say
                    that the man my die
There is mary lou
                    and her baby too
Their both left with dut
                    husband or father
There is no milk
                    she can't hide guilt
And the baby
                    just screams and holler
There is Pearl Mc feal
                    she got hit by the wheels
Of a car
                    with an unknown driver
There's a Preacher Man
                    with a Gun in his Hand
Saying the Devil
                    stole his Bible

                    Hippie Hippie Hippie take this message
And make them listen

I Want To Thank You

Dear God,
  I just want to thank you
      so much
For loving me
    and making me free
Lord for blessing me
    then letting me see
you know the world
    so full of trouble
They are suffering
    killing each other
There are times
    about to lose my mind
Things get so hard
    can't keep from crying
Because of your mercy
    you send someone kind
To stop all my sighing
    they always help me find
A better way to make a day
  to say   Dear God
    I just want to thank you so much
  I'm tired; I've sighed then
    you open the eyes
    of those who are blind
I'm glad I recognize
    the truth before I died
Now that I realize
    you're on my side
And you have paid the price
    for the sins of all men
Righteous devine
    thanks for the sacrifice
        you saved me
When I was dying
    I just want to thank you
      so much

Clown Of Love

The clown of love smiles in pain
Laughter turn to tears
Lonely cries when hugged in vain
For a million years

The heart is filled with desire
Of a thousand names
Love will never yeild when passing by
She must be caught and claimed
I tilled the wills of the soul
Down where love is kept
Touched her softly, gently, slow
Kissed her while she slept

Love awoke, she spoke with me
Tenderly she said
To know me
You must plow deep as the sea
All passion shall be fed

Love may sustain most any clown
Though love must be free
To search and find what must be found
And then go back to sleep

Looking For You

I never had a love before
I thought my heart
 was made of stone
I had affairs by the score
Nothing in life
To call my own

> *no one ever thought to be true to me*
> *no one ever thought to care*
> *I search for love so endlessly*
> *looking for someone who needs me*

> *looking for you — and something to do*
> *feeling blue — when I'm not with you*

You know I've been every where
Trying to find a love so sweet
A girl who knows how to share
Hoping each time that loves for keeps

> *no one ever thought to be true to me*
> *no one ever thought to care*
> *I search for love so endlessly*
> *looking for someone who needs me*

Looking for you — and something to do — feeling blue
When I'm not with you

Open Your Eyes

Inspiration by imgination
                    motivation of a new creation
Just use your mind
                    instead of wasting your time
You will be surprised
                    once you realize
All your thoughts
                    hopes and dreams
Are as real
                    as they seem
Once you conceive and believe
                              I'll guarentee you can achieve
Using the lessons of progression
                              it's geography not
Geometry mixed with trigonometry
                              anthropology and sociology
Psychology has authority
                              biological and sexological
Standerdized, computerized education
                              homogenized, systemized determination
Makes you wise
                    when knowleedge is applied
These are the lessons
                              of progression for connection
Actualization is fascination
                              with revelation of compensation
Contraction with streetology
                              sutraction of stupidology
Is the philosophy you see
                    multipy love and affection
By truth and direction
                    then a great soceity shall be
When you divide
                    all the debauchery you feel inside
Perhaps then civilization
                              inherits a situation to capitalize

Kayla

I believe in santa
                because of people like you
You made a precious dream true
Only pure hearts tread
    where fare hopes share
Secret wishes shall bed
   goodness willl always care
Words can never say
How sweet Kayla feels
   may you have great birthdays
For as long as you may live

Letter Of Love

This is a tale of a kiss and a hug;
First part—
Written in blood; from the depths of
My heart—
This addiction is commissioned by pain;
*   contained;*
in stains of cupid's dart
Life was mellow when we were together,
*   I still feel the thrills you gave*
Then you had to leave
,said obligation you did not need
I begged for you to stay
Remember how I'd pleaded,
*   touched my sorrow with no reason*
Then slowly walked away;

Hello, Hello

How have you been
It's a day and a year
since you were here
Although it seems like forever
am I still your favorite fellow
In your last letter I felt
the presence on someone else
I'm about at wit' end
just a few words
mistakeningly i heard
You found a better friend
This is my letter of love
I loved with all my might
This is my letter, my love letter
the last one I'll ever write
To my love;
You said you loved me only
I thought your love was true
Now my heart is lonely
every night I creid for you
This is my letter of love
my letter to my love
More than a kiss and a hug
I hope you're happy now
if that is what you've found
I've been sighing daily
since you put me down
It you ever need me girl
you know just where I'll be
Sitting on top of the world
been there since you set me free

Looking For Love

Looking for a love I can call mine
A girl that is my very own
Someone fine who will treat me kind
And who won't ever leave me alone
No matter the directions
What is the time or weather
I need a love with affection
That will last forever
She'll be warm in the winter
Nice and cool in the summer
In the fall we'll have a ball
Looking for love, looking for love
What it means to be on the scene
   in the spring
 see what nature bring
I need a love that's true
One and one ain't no fun
Unless they on the same run
I pledge my heart forever
A love my soul can treasure
Soft like cotton
            smooth as satin
Gentle like silk
Someone I can spend my life with
Who will come when I call
            without a moments delay
I want a love that will stay
Together we stand tall
            never betray or go away
Looking for love, looking for love
   who will make me happy
            so much pleasure
I'll be her daddy
            each sweet endeavor
When we touch
We'll exspose a brillant fire

With enough love
To embrace every desire
A love that feel when I feel
And give when I give
A love so real
To be with me as long
As we both shall live
Looking for love, looking for love

Meditation

Sometimes I meditate and
Try to relate
To reflections historiclly timed
To delusions of peace
Illustrated by greif
Embeded and confined to the mind
in search i seek the pleasures
Of releif
May I borrow happiness
From yesterday's dregs
Will gifts of tomorrow
Bear fruits of sorrow
And will peace wait to come when i'm dead
As I gaze into life's mirror
Figures appear more clearer
I wipe a tear from a stained window glass
                   I see happiness by wealth
Peace surmized in death
Incarcerated and chained
To the past

My Fantasy

Is this a special wish for me
How could she be so pretty
Is it a dream or reality
Started holding her tight
Slow dance the entire night
She said can we find a place that's right
So no one else can see our fantasy
Looking in her eyes
Felt something deep inside
She took me by the hand
Said I could be her man
Then bright lights came on
She said come on daddy lets go home
There, we can be all alone

Sunshine

Good morning sunshine
  girl you look so fine
That you can stop time
  without even trying
Now if you half as kind
  as you are devine-
Then you should be mine

This in not a fantasy
You ought to belong to
Me

By natural occasion
And intimate persuasion
It's a real possibility
In pure romance eventually
You loving me like I'm loving you
There's nothig else to do
When hearts are true

The world is much better
When seen together
Each and every day
Love will lead the way
Plant the seed you sew
Water it with kisses
Hugs will make it grow

Sweets For Creeps

Smile for a little while
                              change your style
Forget about the crowd
                              lying, trying; being too loud
There's a fall destined for the proud
                              anybody can be acting foolishly
The field must be plowed
                              before you plant the seeds
Turn a frown into a grin
                              just like you lose you can win
Instead of whinning
                              start your light to shinning
It's so bright it brings
                              light to the darkest night
Although we are born in sin
                              doesn't matter where you start
Allow your righteousnessto begin
                              confess revelations of heart
You shall reap what you sew in the end
                              reject wickedness then depart
Find in your mind things learned
                              devine signs will be discerned
The melodies I shared
                              relevant feelings yet unprepared
You stole my soul
                              with your quest for gold
They come to me naturally
                              pure thoughts evade theivery
Even if you reach the top
                              you'll never enjoy the treats you got
Say you get a million with each crop
                        there'll be no peace
                        in the sweets of a creep

Taxi Cab

Taxi/cab for hire-
take you anywhere
That your heart desire
*   what's your destination*
Give me an indication
Just a wave of the hand
I'll be there by command
Secure the situation
With a grand accommodation
Just jump right in-take a load off your feet
Take you for a spin-let me record the street
Anywhere you wanna go-just let me know
Uptown. downtown, crosstown, out of town
No matter where you bound, I'll take you around
You can pay with denaro, yang or pound
Nothing to fear travel far and near
If you missed your
Train-and you afraid of planes
Never mind I'll get you there on time
The buses are running really slow
Got someplace special you need to go
Give me a sign-I'm easy to find
When you see my light shinning bright on top
A wave of the hand I'm guarenteed to stop
Taxi Taxi-Taxi cab for hire
Take you anywhere your heart desire

The King

Hey Pretty Moma,
 is he treating you right-
If he's not baby
 cut him on back-
Cause I'm here today and
 I'm here to say---
I can do it better
  than any other fellow
My back is strong
   and my wind is long
I'm standing out in the cold
   baby just to get chosed
Baby please be choosing
   so that we can be cruising
Ain't no joking
   I'm sho-nuff smoking
I'm the best
  from East to West
I'm the most
  from coast to coast
From North to South
   without a doubt
I'm your treasure
   your pleasure
I'm the inches that you measure
I'm your passion
   your fashion
Your desire I'll make you happy
I'm the T in Tide
   I'm the P in Pride
I'm the O in the Giggalo
   from the ceiling to the floor
From the window to the door
   Lotti Dotti what you don't know
You better ask somebody
   I'm the King Mr. Everything

A rich girl fortune
> *a poor girl's dream*

I'm the best I know
> *every where I go*

Ladies waiting in line
> *just to keep my time*

I'm the King
> *Mr Everything*

I treat rich girls fair
> *answer a poor girl's prayer*

The Price Of Life

Mistery and fantasy
        caught in the claws of reality
Responsibility---born a slave
        to the strong and the brave
All they live to see
        is a way to be happy and free
Break off the chains
        tied to the brains
Hooked on love
        hooked on drugs
    trying to find a way
        to stop crying
Lost all hope
        in a bag of dope
Those dreams of luxury
        returned home alone and empty
Nothing to eat on the plate
        two days still don't know last time I ate
    hard to have faith
        with no bread to bake
Hard to pray
        hungry all day what can I say
Politicians keep everybody wishing
        listening to lies
While another brother dies
        nobody cares how poor folks live just what you got to give
        in the Getto it's for real
No where to go
        but down you see
When you're down so low
        a blade of grass looks tall as a tree
Soceity created this situation
        there is no condemnation
Lost and forgotten souls
        on the verge of starvation
Time flows where it goes, nobody knows

few survive to grow old

In this world cold as ice

swift and bold sacrifice

Capitalistically, -economically

we are thriving perpetually

Striving sadistically existing, barely

coming to church wacth them work

Hurts inside when you realize

most folks in disguise

Searching to find God

truthfully spiritually starved

Anybody understand

ramifications of an honest man

God alone guides his hand

Happy New Year

Happy New Year
> *, let me make it clear*
Every thing you do
> *take the Lord with you*
Each time you awake
> *open your eyes*
You ought to celebrate;
> *thank God and recognize*
Just a day in the Lords view
> *is like a thousand for me and you*
May the entire year;
> *be full of love and chear*
All you can't understand
> *put it in the Lord's hand*
He's already there
> *to show how much he care*
Whatever you have to do
> *trust the Lord to pull you through*
> *no request is too small*

no wish is too tall

Going For It

I'm going for it each and evey day
I'm going for it so don't get in my way
Everything I do, everything I say
I'm going for it with all of my might
I'm going for it shownuff delight
Everything in life has it's price
Got to reap what you sew
                              you got to sacrifice
  morning and night
                         and that's only right
Let me tell you a story where I come from
You had to learn to fight
                         or you had to learn to run!

I rather be a writer,
                         than to be a streetfighter
Rather be a lover,
                         than a stone cold mugger
I rather be a Player,
                         than to be the City Mayor
Hope inside realize today I arrive for my prize;
I believe, I'll'achieve everything that I need
Once it's conceived, I'll aquire my desire, my thoughts trasnspire, all my
pleasure, all my treasure, my endeavore makes it better;
Going for it going
                         straight to the top
Cause I'm kicking it
            mixing it, using all I got

Valori

Valori I love you
　　　Valori I needed you
Valori no matter
　　　what you do
You make my
　　　dreams come true — ooh---
The first time we met
　　　I can't forget
I held you close
　　　I didn't want to go
As time goes by
　　　I made you cry
I hurt you so
　　　you walked out of my life
For ten long years
　　　through all of the fears
We got to the top
　　　I gave you every thing I got
It was't enough
　　　to make you my bride
You betrade my love
　　　for some other guy
You had my heart
　　　in the palm of your hand
Yeah from the start
　　　you had some other man
Valori I loved you
Valori I needed you
Valori no matter what you do
You broke my heart into
Valori, Valori, Valori

What Do You Want

I thought you wanted me girl
I'm yours whenever you say
It seems you living in a dream world
And you taking life for play

I crave for you so passionately
My love is from the depths of my heart
What good is love for you or me
If love ain't love from the start

Would you even know love
If love was in front of your face
You'd probably let love go love
And never dare to taste

The sweetness is really bitter
Artificial flavored lust
Love is soon your enemy
Because her source is hurt

If love can be a plenty
What is this I feel
How can love be so empty
After being a full course meal

I know you wanted me girl
Though I have no luxury
Love is judge of the world
She must be free and naturally

What Did I Get

Hey brother man, brother right, brother me
Where have you been-
    "I've been to the war and back again"
I know you're glad to be home!
    see how things changed—
Not really, they still running that
    same old game-
Still scheming and jiving
    steady coniving the people
Playing on their minds
    still got my brothers killing
    one another knowing
The only change
    is a change in time
still taking my sisters
    keeping them weeping
Tricking my mother
    she talking about reaping
Got my old man
                in a wheel chair
He can't even walk
    for the heavy burden
        carried on his back
What a blessing it is
        to be right
Got you blind
    so you can't see
Daily exploitation
    of the people and me
Gave you a job, home, security card
    you think you free
Got to bum busfare to the welfare
    from time to time
        when you get there
Still got to wait in line

When A Child Is Born

She's having a baby that's so very fine
She's giving life to one of her kind
Soon to burst forth, with joy and love
A gift from God, designed up above
Through love and care she carries so dear
Man and woman must share to bring it here
This is very precious a seed to last forever
Birth is the greatest and grandest endeavor

Once bred, she'll cherish the child she has born
On this glorious day let Gabriel blow his horn
Nine long months she did her part
Just beginning another stage of heart

Eternity reveal a sacred task undiminished
God has created spiritual paths unending
Graciously conceived love it needs
Every breath it breathes
The source of human soul
Control the mold of our
 species
 wonderful and bold
A blessing from God
The womam and man
Chosen for this job

. . . . *You* . . . .

You're so wonderful-
   like clouds floating by
On a stream in the sky
   and you're so
Beautiful
   I wonder why-you
Sit and sigh
   weep and cry-
All the time
   is it because you're trying hard
To please someone who doesn't care
   no matter how you try to be fair
Justice isn't there
   anywhere-so stop sighing
No matter which way you turn
   will you ever learn
That love will always comand
   the upper hand
For she controls passion and desire
   though man understand
Laws of the land
   and call by name each grain of sand
He will never know
   where love go
When she start
   to die

CPSIA information can be obtained
at www.ICGtesting.com
Printed in the USA
BVHW071925160222
629216BV00002B/211